Theodore Roosevelt

A biography of Theodore Roosevelt, an American President

Table of Contents

Introduction

Thank you for taking the time to pick up this book documenting the incredible life of Theodore Roosevelt.

Theodore Roosevelt was the 26th President of the United States, and proved to be one of the most popular and progressive President's in history.

This book aims to serve as a biography of Roosevelt, documenting his journey in politics, and painting a picture of what the United States was like under his guidance.

In the following chapters you will learn about Roosevelt's early life, how he became involved in politics, how he rose to the position of President, his political views, and what kind of an impact he had in his long career!

At the completion of this book you should have a great understanding of, and a new respect for, Theodore Roosevelt, arguably one of the greatest and most influential American Presidents in history!

Once again, thanks for choosing this book, I hope you find it to be informative and enjoyable!

Chapter 1: Early Life & Before Politics

Weak in body, strong in mind

If you had told a young Theodore Roosevelt that he would one day grow to be the very embodiment of masculinity, strength and resilience in the eyes of the American people, I'm sure that he wouldn't have believed you. This wasn't a failing on his character per se, but a reflection of his physical health from the moment of his conception. From birth, Roosevelt was hampered by a severe form of near crippling asthma. This asthma was so severe that he would often awake in the middle of the night with the feeling of being smothered to death; often forcing him to sleep in a seated position. He would later reflect on memories of his father carrying him throughout the house, patting him on the back as he tried to sleep.

This asthma was so severe that it would have rendered the average sufferer inept; a near cripple in the eyes of the public. But this was Theodore Roosevelt and he was anything but average. By employing a sense of personal drive and ambition that would come to characterize and define his career, Roosevelt became determined to not let this illness hold him back.

'You have the mind, but not the body. You must make the body.'

Wise words, spoken by Roosevelt's father to him at a young age. His father, more than anyone, saw hidden potential in his son and was a key factor in helping him to realize what he could become. It was while hiking in the Alps with his father at the age of eleven that Roosevelt came to realize that by putting his body through extreme bouts of physical endurance, he could combat his asthma. This was so much so that he soon took up a heavy regiment of physical activity, such as boxing and rowing. Over time he built his body to match his mind. This was to such a degree that he never suffered from asthma again.

With his physical body improving dramatically, Roosevelt was thus able to concentrate on building his already prestigious mind. A child of home schooling, Roosevelt gravitated naturally towards the sciences (particularly biology), history and geography. He even authored his own book at the age of nine -- 'The Natural History of Insects.' As he was home schooled, it only stands to reason that he didn't receive the rounded education of others his age, leaving him slightly weaker in the areas of mathematics and classical languages. But, as was a prevailing theme in the life of the ambitious youth, he never allowed this to hamper him. He was a determined student, always striving to do better, regardless of how much harder he had to work to do so.

Thriving at Harvard

The year was 1876 and Roosevelt's natural ambition and high level of intelligence saw him accepted into the prestigious school of Harvard at the tender age of 18. If there was something missing in his youth, it was the comradery and natural competitiveness that abounded for living amongst and studying with peers. At Harvard, surrounded by like minds for the first time, Roosevelt was able to thrive like none could have foreseen. Although he majored in science, he studied mainly the histories and English. He did this as he believed it to be a way of expanding on an area that he wasn't as strong in.

It's important to note too that while in Harvard his physical regime wasn't hampered by his studies. On the contrary, he took up and put his hand to every sport and leisure activity that he could; participating in rowing, boxing and anything else that Harvard had to offer.

As stated, Roosevelt thrived in the atmosphere that Harvard presented. While there, he was a member of the Alpha Delta Phi literary society, the Delta Kappa Epsilon fraternity and even a member of the famed Porcellian Club; one of the most prestigious final clubs in America. As such, Roosevelt graduated Harvard in 1880 at the age of 22. He graduated 22nd out of 122 in the Phi Beta Kappa society for liberal arts and sciences and also graduated Magna Cum Laude; an honor only bestowed upon the most learned of graduates.

There are some men that are destined to succeed in life no matter what they put their minds too. There's no doubt that had Theodore Roosevelt's career path gone a different way than what it did, he would have left a sizeable imprint behind in that field. But for him, a man of that ambition, there was only one role that was large enough for him to fill...

Joining the political realm

Upon graduating from Harvard, Roosevelt decided to study law at Columbia Law School in 1880. Again, this wasn't so much out of a love for the law making process, but a thirst to improve in an area that he saw as critical to his education. However, the more he studied at law, the less he enjoyed it. He was a pragmatic man and he found the variances and inconsistencies in law annoying and irrational. This was most likely the main factor that was caused him to drift from this field of study.

There were two main factors that resulted in his move into politics. The first was from his then girlfriend and soon to be first wife, Alice Hathaway Lee. Like his father had when he was a child, she saw his potential and suggested that he try his hand in politics rather than law.

It's important to note that politics at this time had vastly different career connotations to what it does now. Most politicians were corrupt businessmen who entered the political realm as a means of using the political hammer to further their own personal interests. Roosevelt's realization of this was the second major factor that contributed toward his entering of politics. He saw that it was ultimately these men who ran the country, and he knew that he could do better. What's more was that he knew that he must do better; not just for him but for the sake of the country itself.

It was in 1881 that he began to attend meetings at Morton Hall, the 59th Street Headquarters of New York's 21st District Republican Association. Although this was only a state level political base, once Roosevelt began to attend there was no doubt in his mind what it was that his future held for him. He soon dropped out of Law School, focusing all his ambition on becoming a member of the governing class.

Character

It's important now to take a moment and assess what kind of character made up the man that was to become the 26th President of the United State of America. More than any other President before him, and possibly after, was individual character so heavily intertwined with the way that the most prestigious of offices was run and operated.

When Roosevelt first left for college his father famously said 'Take care of your morals first, your health next and finally your studies.' These were words that Roosevelt was to live by, taking them all the way to the White House.

His extreme level of personal ambition has already been mentioned. As has his natural intelligence and inquisitive mind. But one aspect of him that ruled all other was his moral compass. Throughout his career, Roosevelt always did what he thought was best for country and citizen; regardless of how this may have reflected upon him. He was stubborn, sometimes irrational and always fought to the bitter end. But again, these were all personal attributes that were framed by his strong moral compass. It was a compass that was crafted from birth and came to define a nation.

Chapter 2: Initial Political Inclinations

State Assemblyman

It was 1881 when Theodore Roosevelt first began to ascend the political ladder. After attending a series of meetings at Morton Hall, a platform where he was able to demonstrate his ambition and character in front of his peers, he was quickly put forth as the Republican Party's candidate for the District's House seat in Albany, New York. This was significant as it allowed for him to attend the New York State Legislation meetings and represent his district as an Assemblymen. At the age of only 23, this was a huge step forward in his career and he made sure to participate in the meetings with gusto.

Roosevelt was a passionate candidate and he was able to combine this with his powerful oratory skills to propel himself to the center stage of the legislation meetings, making sure that everyone there knew that his was a name worth remembering.

His primary concern during these meetings was the level of corruption that had been allowed to run rampant through the House. A common occurrence, and one that was very well known, was for party hacks to introduce bills that they knew would be unpopular, thus opening themselves up to bribes to withdraw the bill. Roosevelt, demonstrating the moral verve that his father had instilled within him, made it his mission to weed out this corruption in all forms.

It was on account of this passion and zeal that saw him re-elected into the New York State Assembly in 1882, 1883 and 1884. He was divisive, and his actions weren't always popular. But it was clear that he was determined, and would do whatever it took to get his way. As a result, he was able to cultivate a loyal following of other members of the house who knew that this would be a man to follow.

The 1884 Presidential Election

<u>RUFFLING REPUBLICANS FEATHERS</u>

Up until this point in his career, Roosevelt had been a relative small fry. The corruption cases he had been dealing with were all at the local level and had little, if any real impact on mainstream politics. But his time was soon to come. It was the Presidential Election of 1884 where Roosevelt first truly made his mark on the political sphere. Having been appointed the Speaker of the New York State House, Roosevelt was provided a platform to make his choice for the upcoming Presidential candidate known. The Republican incumbent, President Chester Arthur, was the obvious choice to the majority of the party. Roosevelt however wasn't so sure. A natural reformer and born progressive, he was far more interested in the progressive reforms of Vermont Senator George F. Edmunds. So, despite the possible tarnish this might add to his name, he began to campaign tirelessly for Edmunds.

Despite his campaigning, Arthur eventually lost the nomination to the far more popular candidate, James G. Blaine. The loss of his nominated preference wasn't a concern to Roosevelt. All it did was demonstrate to fellow party members what his approach to politics was like. It was an approach that would come to define his career. Roosevelt didn't care for the party and their combined stance, but rather for the policies themselves. He was willing to put his reputation on the line and go against the majority if he believed that it was the right thing to do.

<u>A SMALL VICTORY</u>

Riding his new found oratory popularity, Roosevelt attended the 1884 GOP National Convention in Chicago. Here he gave a speech to the delegates at the convention, convincing them to nominate a temporary chairman that was against the popular choice put forth by Blaine. Although this was eventually overturned, it again gave him a sampling of politics at a national level and further cemented his name as someone who would do what he thought was right, regardless of what the majority deemed necessary.

FALLING OUT

Roosevelt was at constant ends with the conservative base in the Republican Party and it was only a matter of time before his outspokenness caught up with him. As it was 1884, an election year, it only seemed right that it happened at the end of the Presidential Election campaign.

Roosevelt had managed to paint himself as a reformer. This was to such a degree that when he was campaigning against Blaine for the Presidential Nominee, he allied himself with the newly formed Mugwumps; this was a progressive group that split from the Republican base during the 1884 election campaign. This saw him gain a considerable following amongst likeminded progressives in the Republican Party. However, when his choice of Republican Presidential Nominee didn't get chosen, he was asked if he would back Blaine as the Presidential candidate or move to support the Democrats. Having no choice, he backed Blaine, along with the rest of the Republicans, despite having campaigned so vigorously against him.

This move and supposed hypocrisy saw him loose the support of the progressives in the Republican Party that he had spent the last three years cultivating. With his reputation in tatters, Roosevelt made the bold move to quit politics; believing that he would never again return.

MOVE TO DAKOTA

After his 1884 split from politics, Theodore Roosevelt bought a ranch and moved out west to the town of Medora, North Dakota. Here he learned all things cowboy; from riding a horse to tracking down bandits. It was during this time that Roosevelt managed to shed the scholarly image that he had been branded with in New York and develop the masculine, raw American appeal that would come to define him for the rest of his career.

And, had history gone a little differently, Theodore Roosevelt may have remained out west, living his life as a cowboy. But a series of vicious storms in 1886 saw his ranch fail and with no other choice, he moved back east; returning to his home state of New York.

Chapter 3: Civil Services & War

Civil Service Commission and the NYPD Commission

<u>BACKING OF HARRSION</u>

In 1886 Roosevelt returned to New York City and was instantly approached by local Republican leaders to run for Mayor of New York. Although he knew he wouldn't win, he ran anyway; once again seeing it as chance to make his policies known. And indeed he did lose, but the action was enough to again put Roosevelt's name forward as a person worth watching. His political career was far from over.

The 1888 Presidential Elections were approaching and Roosevelt was certain that the party would again nominate James G. Blaine as their candidate; the very same leader who he had tussled with earlier. But to his shock, Blaine was beaten by progressive Republican, Benjamin Harrison. Seeing this as a chance to back a leader who he actually agreed with, rather than just one the party supported, Roosevelt entered the campaign on his behalf. During this campaign, Roosevelt gave a series of invigorating speeches through the Midwest in his support.

Benjamin Harrison easily won the Presidential Election in 1888 and was thus indebted to Roosevelt.

<u>APPOINTMENT TO UNITED STATES CIVIL SERVICE COMMISION</u>

In return for his help during the Presidential Campaign, Harrison appointed Roosevelt to the United State Civil Service Commission in 1888. Much like his time as a New York Assemblyman, Roosevelt used his time in the United States Civil Service to root out corruption in both government and big business.

Roosevelt was ruthless, irrepressible and overly enthusiastic to the point that he didn't care who he butted heads with, just so long as he believed that the cause was good and just. Without a doubt his biggest and most powerful target was Postmaster General John Wanamaker, who Roosevelt accused of handing out patronage positions for support in the election campaigns; an action tantamount to bribery. Roosevelt's exposure of this, and the subsequent falling out between the two was attributed to Harrison's loss in the 1892 Presidential Election.

NEW YORK CITY POLICE COMMISSIONER

In 1895 the Mayor of New York, a progressive much like Roosevelt, approached Roosevelt and offered him a position on the board of the New York City Police Commission. Roosevelt, seeing it as another chance to enact some much needed reforms, quit his job on the Service Commission and eagerly accepted the role. Within a year Roosevelt had become the President of the Board and set about redefining the way the NYPD operated.

At the time the NYPD were known to be one of the most corrupt police forces in America. As such, Roosevelt went about breaking down and rebuilding the force from the ground up. He first made sure to appoint recruits based on physical fitness and intelligence; as opposed to handouts and political promises. He then went about installing a series of firearm safety procedures and protocols, designed to increase safety. Roosevelt was such a stickler for rooting out corruption and bad police work that he was even known to walk the local 'beats' in civilian clothes, so as to catch officers napping or committing atrocities.

Within two years, Roosevelt had vastly changed the way that the police force operated, entering it into a veritable golden age.

Assistant Secretary to Navy and the Outbreak of War

<u>ASSISTANT SECRETARY TO THE NAVY</u>

The 1896 Presidential Election again saw Roosevelt make his mark. Having backed the eventual winner, William McKinley, he was awarded for his loyalty by being appointed the Assistant to the Secretary of the Navy. Although this was usually a thankless role, Roosevelt was lucky in that his boss, the Secretary to the Navy, John D. Long, was more of an administrator then a reformer. He thus left the majority of decision making in the hands of Roosevelt.

While studying at Harvard, Roosevelt had had written an in-depth study on the effects of the navy and its subsequent victory during the War of 1812. It was during this study that he came to the conclusion that the strength of the navy was directly related to the strength and power of its country. As such, he went about building and improving the American Navy significantly; in particular, concentrating on the construction of battleships.

As it would soon turn out, this was a smart decision.

<u>THE BLOWING UP OF THE USS MAINE</u>

At the time of Roosevelt's appointment to the role of Assistant to the Secretary to the Navy, Cuba was embroiled in a rebellion against their Spanish oppressors. Although America wasn't involved directly, Roosevelt was known to have believed that they should intervene -- helping their neighbors to the south. However, as America had no direct reason to become involved, they remained neutral.

In 1898, the USS Maine was sent to Havana, Cuba as a means of offering some protection from the Spanish to the local American population that resided there. Although this was merely a power play, with no foreseeable consequence, the Maine blew up under conspicuous circumstances on February 15th, 1898. The cause for the explosion is still unknown, but it was enough to turn

America's attention to the war they had been ignoring. What's more, it was the sole cause for swaying public opinion as to America's stance on the war. Soon, cries for retribution were sounded across the country.

The Spanish-American War: The Rough Riders

ROOSEVELT'S INITIAL INVOLVMENT

When the USS Maine was blown up in 1898, America didn't call to arms straight away. In fact, many believed that the Spanish may not have been involved, and fought against joining the war. Roosevelt was not one of these. Without approval from either President McKinley or his superior, Long, Roosevelt quickly ordered the mobilization of the US Navy in the Philippines.

It was a decision that was to prove vital in the war effort. When America did eventually join the war in April 1898, the now ready fleet were able to take advantage of their early mobilization and all but destroy the Spanish fleet at the Battle of Manila Bay.

This battle was crucial as it is seen to mark the end of Spanish dominance in the Americas; the last lingering threat of colonialism. If it wasn't for this victory, America may not have become the superpower that it is today. All of this can be credited to the foresight of Theodore Roosevelt.

THE ROUGH RIDERS

With war declared in 1898, Roosevelt resigned from his position as Assistant Secretary to the Navy, simply because he knew that in that role he wouldn't get a chance to see or be involved in battle. On May 6th of the same year he formed the First US Volunteer Calvary Regiment, a volunteer service which was soon flooded with applicants from Arizona, Texas, New Mexico, and Oklahoma. These applicants were comprised of cowboys, ranchers, gold miners and able bodies that had to be determined physically fit by Roosevelt. As they were primarily from the mid-west, and all true-blood Americans, they were given the moniker 'The Rough Riders,' by the press.

Only a month of training was required, as most of the recruits were already able to ride a horse and fire a gun. The Secretary of War offered Roosevelt the position of Colonel. But as he had no previous military experience, he declined, instead being appointed Lieutenant Colonel and second in command.

The Rough Riders were deployed to Cuba on May 29th, 1898.

ROOSEVELT THE WAR HERO

The Rough Riders partook in three separate and key battles during the Spanish-American War. Without a doubt, the most significant of these was the Battle of San Juan Hill.

This was a battle that Roosevelt and his men were not meant to be directly involved in. Their orders were to march to San Juan Heights where over one hundred thousand Spanish soldiers held their position. As another regiment prepared to attack, Roosevelt and his men were to act as a distraction, driving opposing artillery fire away from the main battle. As battle commenced and the main fighting force remained hidden, Roosevelt became dissatisfied with the danger that this put his men in; as all the fire was now directed on them. Rather than retreating, Roosevelt decided to take the battle directly to the opposition.

In an act that has now been passed into military lore, Roosevelt, from atop his horse, ordered his men charge head first into the battle and opposing gun fire. What should have been a suicide mission instead saw The Rough Riders overwhelm the Spanish forces and claim victory.

In 2001, Roosevelt was awarded by President Clinton the posthumous Congressional Medal of Honor for his bravery and actions during the battle.

Chapter 4: Re-entering the Political Sphere

Governor of New York

A PERSONAL PROMISE

Roosevelt returned to New York in 1898 only to find that word of his heroics in the Spanish-American War had spread considerably. As such, Republican Congressman and 'political boss,' Thomas C Platt, approached Roosevelt about the possibility of running for Governor of New York. This offer was purely political and wasn't out of love for Roosevelt. The Republican's needed a strong candidate to take on the Democratic nominee, and knew that Roosevelt's war record would be an asset.

They were correct in their thinking as Roosevelt narrowly defeated the Democratic nominee and was returned as the Governor of New York in 1899. At this time, the progressive Roosevelt was more than aware of his reputation as a trouble starter, and his lack of popularity amongst the more conservative Republican base. As such, he promised to not make war in the party; opting for unity.

It was a promise that wasn't going to last.

LEARNING OF POLITCS

Perhaps the most significant aspect of his Governorship of New York, and one that would come to have its greatest mark on his future campaigns, was the insight and practice that it gave Roosevelt into the workings of politics on a national level.

As Governor, he learnt much about the national economic issues that currently plagued the country; this was opposed to the state level economic policy that he was only briefly familiar with. He was also exposed to the concepts of trust monopolies and labor relations within the country and what they were doing to the country and its people. These were two key points that were to have a dramatic impact on his time as President.

Another key aspect during this time was the way that Roosevelt began to utilize the media during his tenure in office; perhaps more than anyone had before him. He opted to hold twice a day press briefings, seeing the media as a way to stay connected with the middle-class political system and its voting base. Roosevelt was a natural speaker, with a level of personal magnetism not yet seen by political pundits. By putting his face out there for all to see, he became more popular than ever.

This reliance on the media was to prove revolutionary. Not just for his presidency, but for all future Presidents also.

BREAKING HIS PROMISE

Roosevelt's promise to not start war within the Republican Party didn't last long.

As Governor, Roosevelt was in a position to appoint key individuals of his choice to policy making positions. Platt, the very same who had approached him with the nomination for Governor, insisted that he be consulted on these appointments. He wanted to keep the progressive tendencies of Roosevelt in check. And at first Roosevelt agreed; opting to play nice. But, a natural progressive in a party that hated change, Roosevelt soon ignored his contemporaries, making his own appointments. Again, Roosevelt didn't care about party politics, but country politics, and doing what he thought was best for policy.

This, of course, only served to weaken his image further in the eyes of fellow Republicans. Once again they were reminded that Roosevelt wasn't a 'team player,' like they were so used too. Roosevelt was there to shake up the political system in a way that hadn't been done before. His actions were alien at the time as he was far more concerned with the running of the country and the welfare of his fellow man. The morals that his father drummed into him as a child were an asset that most Republicans deemed a flaw.

The Vice-Presidency

It was 1899 and as the Governor to the most powerful state in the Union, many saw Roosevelt as a possible candidate for the Presidency in the near future. Although the next Presidential Campaign was to begin the following year, Roosevelt had no intention of challenging the incumbent McKinley for Presidency. This was again largely due to policy as Roosevelt backed many of the decisions that McKinley was known to support. However, it is known that Roosevelt heavily contemplated the possibility of running in 1904. This possibility however never had a chance to materialize.

In 1899 the then Vice-President, Garret Hobart died of heart failure. With the election campaign just around the corner, this left the role wide open. At the time, the Vice Presidency was a powerless position, often seen as a step back in politics rather than one forward. With the opening of the role, many suggested that Roosevelt run for the position. He was of course reluctant as he saw his career in its ascendancy stages and feared what the position would do to his image. However, the Republican base, led by Platt who was still dirty about the way that Roosevelt had handled his time as Governor, were eager to get rid of Roosevelt. They thus led a public campaign that heavily pressured him into taking the role.

At the 1899 GOP convention, Roosevelt won the nomination for Vice-Presidency, even though he hadn't asked to be entered. As he was a man of honor, he had no choice but to accept and run alongside McKinley in the election the following year.

THE DEATH OF A PRESIDENT

As the Vice-President to the incumbent McKinley, and with an election coming up, Roosevelt threw himself into the ensuing campaign with his usual gusto and oratory prowess he was known for. Although he wasn't in any way eager for the role, it was still his and like all things in life he would make of it what he could.

Roosevelt made 480 stops in 23 states during the campaign, proving more than a match for the Democratic Presidential nominee, William Jennings Bryan. During the campaign, Roosevelt made sure to emphasize McKinley's peaceful reign, deigning it a golden age for America. This was in contrast to Bryan who was known to have supported the Spanish-American War. As a result of this strategy, William McKinley was returned as President in a landslide, sealing Roosevelt as the new Vice President of the United States of America.

On September 6th, 1901, President McKinley was shot by an anarchist while visiting Buffalo, New York. Although he was at first thought to be fine, he later died on the 14th of the same month.

As was per the constitution there was to be no re-election. Instead, Theodore Roosevelt was sworn in on the same day as the 26th President of the Untied States of America. It was a role that he was to take to, like a duck to water. Never before had a single man been so suited to the position. Ultimately he would go on to change the role of President and in that, change the position that the United States of America had on the world stage forever.

Chapter 5: Redefining the Role of the Presidency

The 'Trust Buster'

<u>THE STATE OF CO-ORPERATE AMERICA</u>

Following the Industrial Revolution and the insurgence of big business, the U.S.A found itself under the control of a series of large co-corporations. These corporations owned and operated everything from railroads to steel refineries. What's more is that each of these corporations were more often than not under the ownership of one, very powerful individual. These individuals wielded extreme influence in the country as they literally controlled the output of their entire industry.

Theodore Roosevelt rightly believed that these tycoon industrialists wielded too much power. And it wasn't just the power that they had which he feared, but it was what they might do with that power. The country was in a position where its economy could literally be crippled by a single individual if they saw fit.

And see fit they more often than not did. These individuals were known to use their immense power to influence political elections and economical bills; effectively controlling the country. Roosevelt saw it as his duty to his country and fellow man to reign in the power of these tycoons.

<u>J.P MORGAN'S RAILROAD'S</u>

Five months into his first term as President, Roosevelt went after millionaire tycoon J. P Morgan. J. P Morgan was an American financier and banker who had his hand in numerous American corporations and industries in the early 1900's. The one that concerned Roosevelt the most was his Northern Securities Company.

The Northern Securities Company was an American railroad trust that was comprised of the Northern Specific Railway, the Great Northern Railway and Chicago, Burlington and Quincy Railroads. With dominant shares in this trust, Morgan effectively owned the entire railroad system in Northern America. Roosevelt saw this as a problem and struck before it was too late.

In 1902, Roosevelt, under the Justice Department, sued Morgan on the terms of the Sherman Antitrust Act. This was a bill passed in 1890 that was designed to specifically combat the creation of monopolies, much like the one that J.P Morgan had created. As it was the first case of its kind, J.P Morgan fought the case adamantly, forcing it to go as high up as the Supreme Court. Later that same year the case was settled, and the Supreme Court forced J.P Morgan to break up the company, relinquishing control of the monopoly.

CONSEQUENCES

As a result of this case, Roosevelt earned the nickname 'trust buster,' although in realty he was more of a trust regulator. As stated, he didn't believe that individuals should have as much power and influence as these tycoons did. Unlike the position of President, they would use their power for personal influence and gain; an action that would rarely be beneficial for the country. His actions in this case were hugely significant when it came to increasing the regulatory powers of the federal government.

This was a theme that was to follow Roosevelt throughout his career. He was adamant that the government should have a greater hand in controlling the welfare of both the people and its country. He knew that only the President could be neutral and do what was best for the country. By the end of his tenure in office he ensured that this was indeed the case for future Presidents.

The Coal Miner's Strike

<u>THE AMERICAN WORKER</u>

Working conditions, and indeed living conditions, in America during the time of Roosevelt's presidency were perhaps the worst that they had ever been. There were no sanitation systems, welfare, or labor laws. If you were poor you would starve, it was as simple as that. This in turn created a situation where the people had to work or they would literally die. One child in five worked in either a sweatshop, a factory, a mine, or a mill. In short, the conditions for the common worker were beyond miserable.

<u>THE STRIKE AND ITS EFFECT</u>

In 1902 the Anthracite Coal Miners went on strike. This was a union that was responsible for the production and acquisition of the majority of the country's coal. And, in the worker's eyes, it was a strike that was long overdue.

The effect that this had on America at the time cannot be understated. Management and labor were in a deadlock. Labor wanted better working conditions where management didn't want to provide the fee's that this would cost. With winter on the approach, the citizens of the country feared for their lives as with no coal readily available, they could freeze to death.

Roosevelt saw this strike as the perfect opportunity for he, as the President, to act on the behalf of the American people in a way that the President never had before. It was only as the President that he was able to take a neutral step back and see things in terms of the national interest of the country. He didn't favor labor or management, but the people.

<u>ROOSEVELT'S ACTIONS</u>

To show that he meant business, Roosevelt first threatened to use the United States Army to seize the coal mines and nationalize the coal industry. This automatically put both management and labor on the back foot. With this power play in check, he was then able to bring the two sides' together, labor and management, and forge a settlement that favored labor over management. In the long run he was a fair man and agreed that the miserable working conditions had to be improved. The laborers were given better pay and fewer hours.

This had huge repercussions on future strikes and labor conditions. First of all, it created a model for future unions to use when trying to improve their own labor conditions. This ultimately paved the way for better working conditions in the future, for all Americans. It was also the first time that the Government became directly involved in a labor strike; an act which further added to the power of the Presidency and its role in federal issues.

Executive orders

One thing that Roosevelt was uniquely famous for was his issuing of executive orders. Before his presidency, Grover Cleveland held the record for the most executive orders issued at 253 during his two terms as President. Roosevelt issued a whopping total of 1081 during his two terms.

This once again highlights the kind of President that Roosevelt was. He saw his role in the Presidency as being there to better the lives of the people and improve the running of the country; despite how this may affect his image amongst his peers. The bureaucratic red tape of politics often got in the way of policy making. On top this, quite often a President's desire to appease his party would influence and affect his ability to make good policy. Roosevelt wasn't of this mind. He did what he thought was morally best, despite how it made him look. Issuing executive orders was in his mind the most efficient way of making good policy that didn't get hampered down by political dealings.

The Role of the Media

It was during his time campaigning for Governor of New York that Roosevelt began to see the role that the media could play in bolstering his image, and when he became President he took full advantage of them in a way that no President had before.

He held press briefings every day, even going so far as to create the Press Briefing Room in the White House, still in use today. These briefings were a great way to keep him in touch with the middle-class, voting base of America, and were a large reason behind his popularity. This was on top of the fact that he was a naturally charismatic, likeable leader. Knowing this, he made sure that his face became the face of the country. It was one of strength and resilience, and came to define America and its people in the early 20th Century.

Theodore Roosevelt enjoyed a long, healthy relationship with the press like no President had before him.

Chapter 6: International Policy

America in post Spanish-American War

POST SPANISH-AMERICA WAR: THE EMERGENCE OF A NATION

Theodore Roosevelt happened to adopt America during a very unique time in its history. With its victory during the American-Spanish War of 1898, the U.S.A had officially graduated beyond infancy and was now considered by many, Roosevelt especially, as a world power. With its navy second only to Britain and a bustling economy, America now had the responsibility to lead, and even civilize the rest of the world in its own image.

It was, in short, the beginning of America's emergence as a world lead. And Theodore Roosevelt was at the forefront.

THE MONROE DOCTRINE

At this same time, European powers were starting to makes moves on their old bases in Latin America. This was usually in an an attempt to force the repayment of loans taken out during colonial times. Roosevelt found these moves to be a strategic threat to the safety and well-being of America. He didn't want any other superpower, save his own, invading the Western Hemisphere. This was now his playground and he wasn't about to let someone else invade it.

With this in mind, and in an attempt to curb further encroachment, Roosevelt invoked the Monroe Doctrine. In true Roosevelt style, he did this on his own accord, without telling congress or even asking permission from Latin America. This was yet another example of the firm hand that Roosevelt believed the President needed to have. Sometimes things needed to be done for the good of the nation and in his mind there was no better cause than the protection of U.S borders.

The Monroe Doctrine was a U.S policy that opposed European Colonialism in the Americas. Originally created in 1823 by President Monroe, it was designed as a way to curb the threat of British Imperialism; especially in regards to the newly formed U.S.A. Although it wasn't necessarily the British that were the problem now, Roosevelt was still able to apply its principles to his own ends.

In order to help apply the Monroe Doctrine to new world order, Roosevelt added a clause to the doctrine knows as the 'Roosevelt Corollary.' What this effectively did was expand the meaning of the text to encompass all European powers, rather than just British ones. Furthermore, it also extended the reach of the text down to Latin America, effectively putting them in the patronage and protection of the United States.

The Western Hemisphere now belonged to Roosevelt and his country, and he would do anything he deemed necessary in order to protect it.

BIG STICK DIPLOMACY

'Speak softly and carry a big stick; you will go far.'

This quote is one associated with Roosevelt and his governing style when it came to invoking and enforcing the principles laid out in the Monroe Doctrine. And indeed, it was one he himself used to justify his future actions when dealing with Latin America.

From now on, America was going to use its 'Police Power,' to enforce good behavior on Latin America. But more than that, it was also going to protect Latin America and its interests. If somebody was going to clean up the neighbor, it was going to be the U.S.A. This wasn't about imperialism or expansion. Roosevelt knew that these were old, colonial policies that had no place in the modern world. It was instead about the assertion of authority; as long as the rest of the world knew who the real power was then that power was safe.

The real strategic significance of this policy was that it didn't necessarily imply any form of violence or action from America, per se. It was purely a way of saying that America was ready to intervene, if it saw fit. America already had one of the strongest Navy forces in the world, backed up by a booming economy. Now, as a growing super power, this threat was more than enough to keep European nations out of the Western Hemisphere.

Theodore Roosevelt did a lot for America during his time as President. But without a doubt, one of his greatest contributions was the way he guided America towards the forefront of the world stage.

The Panama Canal

<u>BACKGROUND</u>

Nowhere were Roosevelt's foreign policy and views on the role of America more on display then in his intervention in Panama.

As mentioned above, Roosevelt was always looking for ways to strengthen America as a country. The best way for this, he believed, was through militaristic expansion, in particular the Navy. Unfortunately, the size of America meant that it was nearly impossible to protect both the east and west coast at the same time. Roosevelt saw this as leaving America exposed and sought to overcome this obstacle.

The Panama Canal was a vision that Roosevelt had concocted, in which a giant canal could conceivably be built through the middle of Panama, thus opening up a waterway that would allow for U.S ships to easily travel from one side of the country to the other. In theory, this was a brilliant idea as it would be the final piece of the puzzle that confirmed America's place as a major sea power.

In practice however, it wasn't to be so simple.

<u>THE CANAL</u>

At the time there were two possible locations for this canal -- Panama and Nicaragua. Without consulting the Colombian Government, Roosevelt got Congress to approve the Panamanian alternative - that was the rights to build a canal through Panama. The initial jubilance of this bill was halted when the Colombian government rejected the proposal. Of course Roosevelt wasn't the type of President, or person for that matter, to simply give up on his idea and move on. As such, a new strategy was formulated.

At the time, the local populace was already in open rebellion against their Colombian oppressors. When they learned of the Colombian Governments rejection of the canal, Roosevelt implied that he would support their rebellion if they would help ratify the treaty. In 1903, Roosevelt, acting under the Monroe Doctrine, sent the gunboat The USS Nashville to Panama in order to help assist with the rebellion. It didn't take long for the rebellion to become successful and with the Colombian Government ejected from Panama, Roosevelt was able to invoke a new treaty with the new government of Panama -- one which saw the construction of the Panama Canal as a top priority.

The construction of the Panama Canal began in 1903, finally being completed in 1914. It was the largest civil engineering project ever undertaken by man and remained as a strategic necessity in America's dominance of the Western Hemisphere right on through to 1997 when it was turned back over to the government of Panama.

<u>ROOSEVELT'S BELIEF</u>

It was Roosevelt's belief that this canal would not only be good for America, but for the entire world. He saw it as his greatest achievement and believed that it was a major contribution towards civilizing the world.

His actions in securing permission to build the canal, and ultimately what he did to the Colombian government are further demonstrations of Roosevelt's governing policies. It wasn't a vanity project, or done in the name of the Republican Party. He was a firm believer that the U.S President had to do what was best for the people, despite how this may make him look. There was a chance that his 'imperialistic' polices may have come off as totalitarian in nature. But he took the risk for the good of the nation, and it paid off.

The Nobel Peace Prize

The Russo-Japanese War was an international dispute fought between Japan and Russia between 1904 and 1905. The war was fought over territory disputes in Korea and Manchuria, both relics of past imperialistic tendencies. When this war began it was expected to be quick and decisive, but went on for far longer than either side had expected. What's more, Japan at the time were considered the underdog. A smaller and 'weaker' nation, they should have been easily beaten. But their defiance of Russia and subsequent victories indicated that they weren't going down easily and could perhaps even win the war in the long run. This resulted in a prolonged and bloody conflict.

Roosevelt saw this war as another chance for America to exercise its new found power and militaristic dominance. In a true demonstration of his governing style, Roosevelt didn't aim to end the war through aggressive means; that is picking a side and joining them in battle. But rather, through negotiations and peace talks.

In 1905 Theodore Roosevelt was able to bring the two sides together and negotiate the Portsmouth Treaty. He was able to do this on two accounts. The first was the string of defeats that the Russian's had suffered. They went into the war the favorites to win, but following a few upsets, they were now on the brink of defeat. Although they wanted a way out, pride would not allow it. There was just no way that they could surrender.

The second reason were the unexpected victories by Japan. As a smaller nation, the war was still taking a heavy toll on them and despite being in the winner's seat, a prolonged conflict would ultimately cripple the country beyond repair. A treaty, one favoring them, would only help to confirm them as the emerging power in the East while at the same time acknowledging that they were the victors of the war. As a result of these factors, both sides eagerly signed the peace accord.

For Roosevelt, the major consequence of his actions in negotiating the treaty was his awarding of the Nobel Peace Prize in 1906. He was the first American to receive the prize and as it stands only the second President in history to be awarded the most prestigious honor.

Furthermore, this only serves to highlight Roosevelt as a pragmatic leader. Given his actions during war and his issuing of the Monroe Doctrine, some may mistake him for a war monger. But this was clearly not the case. As always, he was constantly on the lookout for the best possible option in solving a crisis; peace or war. In this instance he leapt at the chance to negotiate peace talks, knowing it would save countless lives.

Chapter 7: Further Reforms

Federal Food Reforms

<u>THE JUNGLE</u>

In 1906, author Upton Sinclair published the novel; The Jungle. The book was actually meant to be an extreme look at the lives of immigrants in the USA and the way in which they were exploited. It did this through portraying the harsh working conditions they were forced to face; mostly in industrialized cities. Conversely, most readers weren't as concerned for the immigrant workers as they were for the light it shone on the health violations and atrocities within the food industry; most particularly the meat packing industry.

By modern comparisons, the industry health standards were extremely poor. There were zero health regulations to speak of. There were no bathrooms or toilets. Sinks to wash one's hands before handling food were non-existent, and there were even reports of rats and sometimes workers falling into the processes and being grinded up with the meat.

Following the outcry from the publication of this book, Roosevelt saw it as another chance for the federal government to become involved on behalf of the consumer and the American people.

<u>MEAT INSPECTION ACT AND PURE FOOD AND DRUG ACT</u>

At first, Roosevelt was naturally hesitant to deem the 'facts' presented in the book as just so. So first, he sent the current Labor Commissioner and a social worker to inspect a meat packing plant in Chicago. Even though the owners of the plant learnt of the impending inspection, and worked to prepare the plant beforehand, the inspectors were still disgusted by what they saw.

In 1906, Roosevelt pushed for Congress to pass the Meat Inspection Act. This called for the government to have a personal hand in the inspection of meat packing plants across the country. However, Roosevelt saw that this wasn't going far enough as it wasn't only the meat packing industry that committed such harsh violations of health laws. He thus followed the Act up with the Pure Food and Drug Act. This saw all bases covered and had remarkable effects on food regulation policy.

Land Conservation Acts

<u>VIEW ON NATURAL CONSERVATION</u>

America was changing. With industrialization in full swing, the majority of the American people had begun to migrate from the mid-west to the larger cities. Consequently, the cowboy image of America was fast on the decline and so was its natural landscape. Roosevelt, being the ex-cowboy that he was, began to notice this on some of his expeditions to the west. And it wasn't just their abandonment that worried him, but their destruction.

He believed, and rightly so, that the wilderness and the grand beauty that it portrayed, was the heirloom of the U.S.A. They were the backbone and character of America and needed to be preserved for the sake of his children and their children.

<u>REFORMS</u>

Roosevelt is now considered to be the first conservationist President. In 1902 he passed the Newlands Reclamation Act. This encouraged the construction of dams by the federal government to help irrigate small farms, while also placing 230 acres of land under federal protection.

Then, in 1906, Roosevelt passed the Antiquities Act. This gave him the initial authorization he needed to halt the destruction of the American landscape; a destruction that was slowly taking place in favor of industrialization and expansion.

During his tenure, Roosevelt managed to preserve 230 acres of land, 51 bird reserves, 4 game reserves, 150 national forests, and 18 U.S National Monuments, such as the Grand Canyon. Again, this only goes to demonstrate the type of leader that Roosevelt was. A hunter by nature, he was more concerned with preserving life then destroying it if he saw it as good for the nation.

Chapter 8: End of Presidency

The 1904 Election

As Roosevelt wasn't technically elected for the Presidency in which he was currently residing, it was unknown as to whether he would be nominated by the Republican Party to run in the 1904 Presidential Election. In fact, the Republican Party Chairman, Mark Hanna, wasn't as open to the idea as most, even hinting at the idea of putting forth another name. From the Republican's standpoint this was justifiable as Roosevelt was never popular in his own party, with his progressive tendencies ruffling the Republican feathers on more than one occasion.

Roosevelt knew this to be the case and thus went about ensuring that he wouldn't be undone. To counter Hanna, Roosevelt and Ohio State Senator Joseph B Foraker, expertly outmaneuvered him by calling on the Ohio State Republican Convention to nominate Roosevelt. They did so with the gusto that only a President as popular as Roosevelt could conjure, making their preference for him well known. As Hanna didn't want to be seen as breaking from the party, he had no choice but to back Roosevelt too.

Roosevelt's progressive policies and the way that he governed for the people and the country as a whole, rather than just for his party, ensured that his popularity was beyond measure. This was on top of his expert use of the media to promote his own image amongst the working class as a relatable, approachable President that was the very embodiment of American ideals. As such, the people ensured that he won the 1904 Election by the largest margin ever seen in a US Election.

He was overjoyed with the result, but in keeping with tradition he announced that this would be his final term as President. It was a statement that he would very soon regret having made.

The Grooming of Taft

As he had promised not to run a third term, Roosevelt found himself in somewhat of a bind when his second term came to an end. Still relatively young, he was more than physically and mentally capable of staying in the Presidency. Furthermore, a lot of the policies that he had enacted, plus the path that he had set the country on, were still taking place. He knew that if a Democrat was to win, or a conservative Republican, then all of his work would be for naught. In order to counter this problem, Roosevelt believed it prudent that he insert his own man into the race, thus ensuring that the ship wouldn't sink.

After cycling through a handful of candidates, he fell on his current Secretary of War, William Howard Taft. Taft had already served under Presidents Harrison and McKinley, and he was also one of Roosevelt's closest friends. Furthermore, he was seen as the type of man that could get things done. Not an innovator, but a hard worker who had always been reliable. To Roosevelt he seemed like the perfect choice to fill the role.

Although Taft wasn't in the same league politically as Roosevelt, he easily won the 1908 election for President. This is perhaps just another example of how popular Roosevelt was with the people. It was well known that Taft was the candidate of choice, personally picked by Roosevelt. This, as well as running on a progressive campaign while following his predecessor's policies, meant that there was no way he could lose. And indeed, with Taft returned as the 27th President of the United States of America, Roosevelt could leave the party knowing that it was in good hands.

Chapter 9: Breaking from the Republican Party

Schism in the Republican Party

<u>FALLING OUT WITH TAFT</u>

While Taft ascended to the most powerful position in the free world, Roosevelt went on a hunting expedition through Africa, blissful in the knowledge that the country and all the hard work that he had completed over the last eight years was in safe hands. Roosevelt however greatly underestimated Taft's governing style, and it was an underestimation that he would soon regret. Where Roosevelt used the Presidency as a platform to construct ground-breaking policies, Taft believed that the role of the President was simply to uphold the constitution and nothing more -- almost a figurehead position. As a result of this view point, slowly but surely, a lot of the work that Roosevelt had done during his time on the veritable throne was disappearing and being dismantled.

One of the promises that Roosevelt had made Taft take was that he would consult with Roosevelt about any cabinet changes and appointments that he was to make; most of the cabinet having been placed there under Roosevelt. When Roosevelt returned from Africa, he was most distressed to see that Taft had not only made numerous changes, but had failed to consult with him on any these. What was even worse was that Taft was beginning to revert back to the more conservative policies that used to dominate the Republican Party before Roosevelt came along.

So, returning to America and not liking at all what he was seeing, Roosevelt began his bid to re-enter politics. Of course there is speculation as to whether this was done out of malice and irritation at being ignored, or because he believed that it was for the good of the country. As was his style, it is most likely that his actions were purely motivated by patriotic principles, believing that Taft was acting against the interests of the country.

As he was returning from a large period of inaction, Roosevelt first attempted to renter the political sphere at the state and local level. In August of 1919 he gave a series of speeches which were without a doubt the most radical and progressive of his career. The speeches themselves weren't that important. What was important was what they signaled; that Roosevelt and Taft's policies were at polar opposites. Taft had effectively become his own man and Roosevelt wasn't happy about it.

WEAKENING THE REPUBLICAN PARTY

At the time of Roosevelt's return to politics, the Republican Party 'boss' was William Barnes Jr, a conservative like Platt before him. Roosevelt, seeing him as a threat, began a vigorous campaign to wrestle control of the party from him. As Roosevelt was now an outsider this would have been hard enough. But it was made even more difficult when Taft backed Barnes over Roosevelt. Nonetheless, Roosevelt continued his campaign amongst the Republicans.

It was during this campaign by Roosevelt that the 1910 State Elections were taking place. These elections would determine which party had the most power in Congress; Republicans or Democrats. These elections were a very delicate time for both parties, as they needed to show unity in order to win seats. As such, it was unarguably Roosevelt's continual maneuvers within the Republican Party, and in-fights with Taft and Barnes, that weakened the party in the House of Congress, resulting in them losing the elections for the first time since 1894.

Despite all of this, Roosevelt was still continually critical of Taft's polices; only serving to further the rift between the two men and split the Republican Party even more so. The party had descended to the weakest point it had been at in over fifteen years.

For all of Roosevelt's positive attributes, he was insatiably stubborn to the point of pigheadedness. Although in his eyes he was doing the right thing for the good of the nation, the way he went about it was at times foolish and ultimately reductive.

The Republican Primaries of 1912

It was unknown as to whether Roosevelt was going to run for the Presidential nomination in 1911 or not. Indeed, he was very coy about it, hinting that if it were tendered to him then he would accept, but never making a solid promise on the fact. All the while he was still continually critical of Taft's role as President; this was despite of how it had affected the State Elections. He was in fact so critical that he even began to declare that only he could bring the Republican Party back from the brink of destruction that Taft had tendered it to. And as such, he announced his intent to run for President shortly before the primaries began.

The 1912 primaries were significant in the fact that this was the first time that they had been used to their fullest extent. More often than not, the party's top choice for President would ascend to the role, regardless of how many hopefuls put their name forward. This was always in a bid for unity within the party. But the unity was now long gone. And on top of this, the majority of Republicans wanted Taft in the role, but the stubborn Roosevelt wasn't going to step down. Consequently, a full campaign to see who would run on the Republican ticket was soon underway.

The two nominees toured the country extensively, drumming up support amongst fellow Republicans as they tried to secure the nomination. The campaign was exceptionally close as Taft did well in the southern states, as was expected, while Roosevelt did well in the mid-west. In the end however it was Taft, being the party's choice, which was the cause for his win. He had more party delegates in his support and thus secured the nomination for Republican Party President going into the 1912 elections.

This should have been the end of Roosevelt's political career. And for the average man it just may have been. But that was never his way. For the good of the country, he still had more moves to make.

The Bull Moose Party

<u>BREAKING FROM THE PARTY</u>

Although Roosevelt had lost the primaries he still had a very strong backing from the progressives in the house. This was to such a degree that they urged him to leave the Republican base and create his own Progressive Party. Although Roosevelt was sure that he wouldn't win, and even more sure that the Democrats would, he accepted the suggestion; breaking from the Republicans and creating the Progressive Party. Again, this needs to be seen in light of what kind of a politician Roosevelt was. He wasn't doing this for his own ego, but because he believed that his policies were best for the country and needed to be put into the public sphere.

Although the party was officially called the Progressive Party, it was popularly known as the Bull Moose Party. This clever name was conceived after the press asked if Roosevelt was fit to run and he replied that he was as fit as 'a bull moose.' And indeed, his campaign model showed that he was just that. One such example was while he was campaigning in Milwaukee, Wisconsin. About to give a speech, he was shot in the chest. Rather than rush to the hospital as he ought to have, he stayed put and delivered the 90-minute speech he travelled there to make. Roosevelt would let nothing get in the way of policy and good governance.

<u>THE ULTIMATE EFFECT</u>

Although the intent was admirable, the effect of his running as a third party candidate had a considerable, and predictable, effect on the 1912 Presidential Election.

As was predicted, even by Roosevelt himself, his entrance into the election campaign split the vote considerably. The Democratic nominee was the very popular Woodrow Wilson and it would have taken a unified party to beat him; if at all. This was on top of the fact that Wilson was also a progressive, meaning that a lot of the Democratic voters who may have voted for Roosevelt's progressive regime were convinced to cast their votes in favor of Wilson.

In the end Wilson won the 1912 Presidential Election with 43% of the popular vote, in contrast to Roosevelt's 27% and Taft's 23%. Wilson was the first Democratic President in over 15 years, leaving Roosevelt more on the fringes of the government than he had ever been.

Chapter 10: Post-Politics

World War One

After the 1912 election loss, Roosevelt continued to dabble in politics, if only briefly. In the 1914 State Elections, Roosevelt made several appearances for the Progressive Party, using his influence and name recognition to make sure that their policies were heard. Many even envisioned him running again in the 1916 elections. And indeed he may have if the Republican nominee hadn't been Charles Evans Hughes. Hughes' policies were largely similar to those of Roosevelt's, and thus he saw no reason to oppose him. He knew that doing so would again only split the vote, opting to again do what was right for the country.

<u>WOODROW WILSON</u>

At the outset of World War One, Roosevelt without a doubt put his support behind the Allies, as did the majority of America, including President Wilson. How Wilson and Roosevelt differed was in what they thought should be done. Roosevelt believed that America should intervene in the war, especially following Germany's controversial submarine warfare which saw the sinking of unmanned vessels -- a veritable war crime. Wilson however opted to remain neutral from the war to begin with.

In 1917 America finally joined the war, but this still didn't manage to quell the tension between Wilson and Roosevelt. Upon announcing their intention to join the fight, Congress gave Roosevelt the authority to raise four divisions of soldiers in a similar style to the Rough Riders that he had recruited for the Spanish-American War. Woodrow Wilson though, being the Commander-In Chief, decided that he wouldn't send Roosevelt and his men to the front lines. Instead he sent an American Expeditionary Force. Roosevelt was thus forced to disband the volunteers. Wilson had effectively neutered Roosevelt in the eyes of the people.

Although it is well documented that Roosevelt was actually impressed with many of Wilson's domestic policies, supporting that majority of them, he was at arms with Wilson constantly over his handling of the war. It was this final refusal to allow him and his recruits to see battle that led him to relinquishing his praise of Wilson entirely, returning once and for all to the folds of the Republican Party.

A Possible Return to Politics

Oddly enough, it was Roosevelt's continual attacks on Wilson that helped propel him back into the popular sphere. His biggest attack on Wilson was in regards to his 'Fourteen Points.' These points were a set of principles to be used when suing for peace with Germany. Although they were seen as fair and just to most, Roosevelt felt that they were far too soft on the aggressive power, calling instead for the unconditional surrender of Germany and nothing more. This stance, as well as a series of passionate speeches he gave against Wilson, helped the Republicans win back a majority seat in Congress in 1918. This was the first time they held a majority seat since Roosevelt had been responsible for their loss in 1910.

Roosevelt had never been more popular with the Republicans. Although he was still progressive, his attacks on the Democratic leader was seen as making him the lesser of two evils, and slowly the party began to fall in line behind him. This was to such a degree that most believed he would run for President in the 1920 Presidential Elections. And what's more, that he could win it.

Death of a lion

The night of January 5th, 1919 Roosevelt was said to have been suffering from breathing problems. But by the time the physician had treated him he was believed to have been feeling better and went to bed. Between 4am and 4:15am Roosevelt died in his sleep. A blood clot had detached from a vein and travelled into his lungs, smothering him while he slept.

It was a simple death. A quiet death. If he had been awake, there is no doubt that Roosevelt would have put up a fight to the bitter end. For someone who lived their life with such aggression, being the very embodiment of the 'never say die' attitude, it is perhaps appropriate that this was the way that Roosevelt went.

Chapter 11: His Legacy

Reshaping the Image of America

Without a doubt, Roosevelt's biggest achievement while President was the way that he redefined America's role on the world stage. When Roosevelt was sworn in as President, America was still seen by most as a young, up and coming country. By the time he left, it was a veritable power house that would have untold influence on future world events.

Some may say that Roosevelt was lucky in that he inherited the nation just after its victory in the American-Spanish War. It was this victory in the war that ejected the last of the colonial powers from the neighborhood, leaving America as the sole contenders for the Western Hemisphere. But in fairness to Roosevelt, it was solely due to his actions that America came to dominate that part of the world like it did.

This began with Roosevelt's belief that a strong navy was pivotal in strengthening the country's borders. It was because of this that he poured countless resources into the navel program, building it to the point where it was second only to Great Britain. Next, by building the Panama Canal, he ensured that America could act at a moment's notice on behalf of all the countries that it surrounded; no longer hampered by its immense size.

Following on from this strengthening of the navy, Roosevelt was able to enact the Monroe Doctrine with absolute impunity, knowing that there wasn't a power that could stop him. Using 'Gun Boat Diplomacy,' now made possible by the increased naval size, America slowly but surely expanded its reach in the Pacific.

By the time Roosevelt left the office of President, the country was stronger than it had ever been before. There were few that could match it for physical strength, and even less who would want to. This paved the way for America to become the powerhouse it is today.

Defining the role of the President

A second aspect of his Presidency that can't be understated were the measures he took that helped define the role of the President, and more importantly, what could be achieved under this role.

Before Roosevelt took office, the role of President was more of a figurehead position, one that was often subject to the whims of the party that it was a part of. Roosevelt however wasn't the type to let others, especially political pundits, tell him how to run his office. What's more, Roosevelt more often than not disagreed with what his party thought as best. Where they wanted to control policy, Roosevelt wouldn't let them; pushing his own ideas ahead of theirs.

When looking at the way that Roosevelt handled domestic issues, such as the coal miners' strike and even the food regulation bills that he passed, it's important to note that what he was doing at that time was revolutionary. Never before had a President taken a personal interest in such small domestic issues. These were usually dealt with at the state level, or in house. But Roosevelt knew that as President he was in a unique position to act on behalf of the citizens and the entire country. By stepping in and personally handling these situations himself, Roosevelt increased the role that federal government was to have in state issues.

Furthermore, he was the first President to realize the important moral position that the President had. The President was in a sense the representative of the people, in the eyes of America and the world. He saw it as his job to properly articulate and influence American policy and what's more, to mobilize the people behind this policy. He used the Presidency to redefine the American moral compass, helping the country to grow into the nation it is today.

A finally, his influence on the media needs to be mentioned. The national media was still in its infancy when Roosevelt took office, and he made sure to utilize it to its fullest. By holding daily press briefings, he ensured that the people were as involved in the political dealings of his party as he was. Politics was no longer a rich man's game, but one that the entire nation could get behind. And at the head of it all was the President.

The Square Deal

Finally, it would be hard to talk about Roosevelt and his time as President without mentioning his most famous policy making stance; the 'Square Deal.'

The Square Deal was the cornerstone policy that made up his time as President, laying the foundations for the majority of his progressive policies. These policies can be boiled down to three key points; consumer protection, the conservation of natural resources and the control of corporations. Inclusively, they are known as the 'Three C's.'

For consumer protection, he stressed the importance of equality and equal opportunity in the workforce. This can be seen pretty clearly in everything from his dealings with the coal miners' strike right on through to his issuing of the Pure Food and Drug Act. His concern for the conservation of the American wilderness is evident in his passing of the Antiquities Act. And finally, the control of corporations is more than evident when looking at the way he dealt with trusts and big corporations when he first entered the Presidency.

Roosevelt was a progressive in a party that stressed conservatism. His square deal is clear evidence of this as he sought change and reform for the betterment of the country and its people; despite what the majority of his party wanted. His ability to make these changes, while still remaining popular with the voting base and many in his party was testament to what a President could do if they applied themselves.

The way that he attacked the Presidency, with clear goals in mind that were aimed at the betterment and advancement of the people and the country as a whole was a model that future Presidents would use when running the most powerful country on earth. It's what made America the nation that it is today. If nothing else, this was his greatest legacy.

Conclusion

Thanks again for taking the time to read this book!

You should now have a good understanding of Theodore Roosevelt, his incredible life, and the impact he had on the future of the United States.

If you enjoyed this book, please take the time to leave me a review on Amazon. I appreciate your honest feedback, and it really helps me to continue producing high quality books.

www.ingramcontent.com/pod-product-compliance
Lightning Source LLC
Chambersburg PA
CBHW061239030726
47595CB00004B/1611